ABC

of PEOPLE and THINGS in the BIBLE
Parents/Teachers Manual 1

ABC
of PEOPLE and THINGS in the BIBLE
Parents/Teachers Manual 1

BY
©Oluwakemi O.Ola-Ojo
2011

ABC of People and Things in the Bible
(Parents/Teachers Manual Book 1)
ISBN –978-1-908015-04-4

© 2011 by OLUWAKEMI O. OLA-OJO
All publishing rights belong exclusively to Protokos Publishers.

Published by:
Protokos Publishers
PO Box 48424
London
SE15 2YL
United Kingdom.
Website: www.protokospublishers.co.uk
E-Mail: admin@protokospublishers.co.uk

Cover design by **DM Audiovisuals**
www.dmaudiovisuals.com

Printed in the United Kingdom. All rights reserved under International Copyright Law. Contents and/or cover may not be reproduced in whole or in part in any form without the express written consent of the Publisher.

ACKNOWLEDGEMENT

I am most grateful to God who through Jesus Christ came into my life at the age of eight and the blessed Holy Spirit who has since been my teacher, friend and mentor.

I am grateful to God for my family, friends and those in the various Children Ministries who has been a blessing and encouragement to me over the years.

Thanks to my Editor, Mrs. `Sumbo Oladipo for doing a marvellous work and on time.

Thanks to all who found time to read and comment on this book for their invaluable comments and encouragements.

Thanks to the management of DM Audiovisuals for providing the distinct and unique covers for this series.

And finally, I thank Protokos Publishers for the excellent work they have done and for making my dreams come through in publishing and marketing my books.

Parents/Teachers Manual

To:

The Holy Spirit:
Who helps us to understand
and obey God.

CONTENT PAGE:

Acknowledgement		v
Dedication		vi
Aim of the Series		viii
Guide to the Parents/Teachers		xi
A:	Adam	14
B:	Boaz	17
C:	Caleb	20
D:	David	23
E:	Enoch	26
F:	Felix	29
G:	Goliath	31
H:	Hannah	34
I:	Isaac	37
J:	Jesus Christ	40
K:	King Asa	43
L:	Lydia	46
M:	Moses	49
N:	Noah	52
O:	Onesimus	55
P:	Peter	58
Q:	Queen of Sheba	61
R:	Rebecca	63
S:	Shepherds	66
T:	Timothy	69
U:	Uriah	72
V:	Virgin Mary	75
W:	Wise men	78
X:	X-Ray	81

Parents/Teachers Manual

| Y: | Yaweh | 84 |
| Z: | Zacchaeus | 87 |

Opportunity to be Born Again   90
Other Books   93
Useful Web sites and addresses   109

MY ABC OF PEOPLE AND THINGS IN THE BIBLE

EXPECTED AUDIENCE:

This series is targeted at children through the:
- Parents.
- Teachers in Christian Primary Schools.
- Teachers in Bible Clubs.
- Teachers in after School Clubs.
- Teachers in the Sunday School.

AIM OF THE SERIES:

- To offer the opportunity for parents to have structured reading with the child.
- To offer the opportunity for the child to read with the parent from the Bible from an early age with the hope of getting the child interested in the Bible and God.
- The child reading to the parent hopefully will help to boost the child's reading confidence.
- To foster parent/child bonding and good childhood memories as they read/study the Bible together.
- When used at home, it provides opportunity for learning during the week as opposed to Sunday school learning.

- This learning hopefully will complement or reinforce Sunday school learning where the book is used as a teaching guide.
- To stimulate learning of Bible stories and people in the Bible (for the 6 - 8s) applicable to the child using the alphabets.
- To provide reinforcement of what is learnt through the suggested exercises.
- To provide an early opportunity for the child to learn about God and God's creation using Bible stories.
- To provide the child the opportunity to self-express his/her creativity in reading, writing, drawing and colouring.
- To provide an early opportunity for the child to learn about people and events in the Bible.
- To provide an early opportunity for the child to become saved and to learn to grow in Christian faith.
- The exercise section is for the parent to work with child through the week.
- To provide the forum for the child to ask questions relating to God, the Bible and the Christian faith, faith in God, fear and how to deal with it, etc.

There will be an accompanying workbook for the child that will help the child in learning to read, write and draw whilst at the same time reinforcing the lesson.

GUIDE TO THE PARENTS/TEACHERS

- Take time to read the story yourself beforehand and pray.

- Parents are the first and most important teachers. They are God's representative to the child so they should live what they teach.
- Ideally parents should know the ability and capability of their child and, each lesson should be adapted to the child.
- Both parents if possible should be involved, perhaps taking it in turns.
- Children have so much to learn in their lifetime and parents can share their experience as they read together.
- Remember to allow time for child's questions.
- Praise child for his/her effort, however little as he/she goes through the workbook.
- Make the learning fun and consistent.
- Children learn at different speed, adapt teaching to child's ability and capability.
- Depend on the Holy Spirit after good preparation.
- The same lesson can be adapted to the age and capability of any younger sibling in the same family.
- Aim is to teach child one alphabet per week, reading the story to the child from the children's Bible or use simplified versions of the Bible e.g. NIV, if a Children's Bible is not available.
- Use child's name wherever child is written in the book i.e. make it personal to the child.
- Use the accompanying workbook for the child learning to read, write, draw and colour.

Focus on one side of the story per day e.g. A is for Adam:

Day 1: You may choose to talk about God, who He is, what He does or can do.

Day 2: Identify all that God created in your home and outside your home.

Day 3: Discuss the role/need of each creation e.g. sun to shine, wind to give us air, man to worship God and have dominion over all other creation.

Day 4: Discuss how God made each one of us unique and look for good traits in your child. God has a plan/reason for everyone He created including child.

Day 5: God made the man and the woman, identify with child some male and female members of your family or in your church or neighbourhood.

Day 6: God saw that everything He created was good including child.

Day 7: God rested. God wants us to rest especially after hard work.

- Encourage child to use the accompanying workbook as it reinforces the lesson.
- Where there are more than seven lessons for the alphabet, the parent/teacher should choose the most appropriate for the child.

Children have short concentration time therefore:
- Make the story interesting.
- Keep it simple and straight to the points.
- Teach each lesson at least twice in a particular week.

- Read the story from the Child's Bible at bedtime throughout that week to reinforce knowledge.
- Relate the Bible lesson for that week as much as possible to the daily events around the child. e.g. in the above keep identifying with child all that God created that you both can see, relating it to child's use e.g. the sun keeps us warm and thank God for each creation.
- Encourage the child to read from his/her workbook.
- Encourage the child to practice writing in his/her workbook
- Let the child self express his/her drawing and creative skills. The picture drawn can be coloured on a different day during that week.
- As much as possible, give the child a positive and encouraging feedback on the reading, writing and drawing.
- Allow the child a break if he/she is tired, whilst working on the workbook.

Remember Romans 10:17 – faith comes by hearing and hearing by the word of God (Deuteronomy 6:1-9; Proverbs 22:6).

A is for Adam, the first man on earth.

Read: Genesis 1:26 - 30.

Points:
- God created the heavens and the earth.
- God made man.
- Adam was the first man that God made.
- God made man to have fellowship/friendship with God.
- Man is to rule over all of God's creation.
- God loves each person including (child's name).
- God looks at (mention child's name) and says he/she is beautiful/handsome.
- God made men and women.

Exercise:
- You may choose to talk about God, who He is, what He does or can do.
- Identify all that God created in your home and outside your home. Help the child to identify other things around him/her that God made, relating it to the child's use e.g. the sun keeps us warm and thank God for each creation.

- Discuss the role/need of each creation e.g. sun to shine, wind to give us air, man to worship God and have dominion over all other creation.
- Discuss how God made each one of us unique and look for good traits in your child.
- God made the man and the woman, identify with child some male and female members of your family or in your church or neighbourhood.
- God saw that everything He created was good including child.
- God gave the child two hands to hold, draw, paint, write, two ears to hear, two eyes to see, legs to walk, mouth to talk, eat and sing etc.
- God has a plan/reason for everyone He created including child.

Parent/Teacher's additional note:

B is for Boaz, the great grandfather of King David.

Read: Ruth 4:17

Points:
- Boaz was a wealthy man.
- Boaz was a kind man.
- Boaz was a generous man.
- Boaz was a caring/loving man.
- Relate the above to God's fatherly love to His children.

Exercise:
Briefly in an uncomplicated way:
- Tell the child about his/her or any forefathers using any pictures if available.
- Together with the child draw or make a family tree explaining to child who a great grandfather is.
- What it means to be wealthy having enough for one's need and much more from which the person can help others financially or materially.

Let the child know:

- That it is God's will for His children to be wealthy.
- What it means to be kind and why we should be kind.
- What it means to be generous and why we should be generous.
- What it means to be a caring person.
- Identify with the child someone who the child can show kindness to and help the child to extend kindness to the person or organisation e.g. sharing his/her toys, giving some toys away etc.
- Ask child what will he/she do with his/her God's given wealth.
- Pray for and with the child that God will help him/her to be wealthy and on the identfied reason for wanting to be wealthy.

Parent/Teacher's additional note:

Parents/Teachers Manual

C is for Caleb, the good reporter and wonderful warrior.

Read: Numbers 13:1- 33

Points:
- God promised to give Canaan to the Israelites.
- The people needed to prepare to enter and take over Canaan.
- 12 spies were sent to check Canaan.
- Caleb was among the 12 spies.
- Caleb and Joshua brought good report.
- Caleb trusted God to help them against the giants, the sons of Anakim.
- Caleb chose to be on God's side.
- Caleb spoke the truth even though it was unpopular.

Exercise:
Briefly help the child to:
- Understand how to trust God.
- Understand the importance of speaking the truth.
- Know that God wants every child to tell the truth always [Proverbs 22:26, 12:17a].
- Know that God rewards those who tell the truth.
- Acknowledge positively every truth the child speaks.
- Know that trusting God is a choice for every person to

make including child.
- Know that it is better to be on God's side than on wrong people's side.

Note:
It is important that the Parent/Teacher realise that the child is watching them and children tend to know if and when the Parent/Teacher is not telling the truth.

Parent/Teacher's additional note:

D is for David, the man after GOD'S own heart.

Read: 1 Samuel 16:2- 22

Points:
- David looked after the sheep as a small boy very well.
- Alone with the sheep, David learnt how to talk to God about his fears and hopes early in life.
- David was always praising God and praying to God.
- David learnt how to trust God early in life.
- David learnt to use the sling.
- David played musical instruments whilst looking after the sheep.
- David sang to God as he watched over his father's sheep.
- David later became a king in Israel whom God loved.
- David wrote many songs and psalms to God.
- David knew how to say sorry to God when he was wrong.

Exercise:
Using child's name, help the child to know that:

- God loves child.
- Child can talk to God at this age, anywhere and on anything.
- God will protect child even when Dad and Mum are not there.

- Child has a purpose in God's plan for the world.
- God is able to use child in whatever area/field he/she chooses.
- God honours those who trust in Him including child.

Help the child to :
- Form and sing a song unto the Lord.
- Discover his/her talent and encourage him/her on how to use it for God.
- Learn to praise God always.
- Know how to say sorry to God and others when he/she is wrong.

Parent/Teacher's additional note:

E is for Enoch, the man who walked with GOD and never died.

Read: Genesis 5: 21.

Points:
- Enoch loved and believed God.
- Enoch obeyed God throughout his life.
- God took Enoch so he didn't die.
- Using John 3:16, Revelation 3:20 in an uncomplicated way, help the child to understand the need for and, how to become born again or God's child.
- Give child the opportunity to be saved.
- Using child's name, tell child that he/she believes in Jesus and will live with God forevermore or in heaven when he/she dies.
- Encourage child on how he/she can walk with God even now.

Exercise:
- Using child's name, say (mention child's name) loves God, believes in God and will obey God.
- God loves (mention child's name) too.
- God has a place prepared with Him for those who walk with Him.
- God rewards obedience to Him.

- Let the child know that it is possible for him/her to obey God and be God's friend.
- Together with the child identify the ways the child can walk with God e.g. by talking to God in prayers and singing.
- By listening to God and obeying Him.
- By showing love to all the other people.
- By being conscious not to destroy other species unnecessarily.

Parents/Teachers Manual

Parent/Teacher's additional note:

F is for Felix, the governor.

Read: Acts: 23 – 24:27

Points:
- Felix was a governor.
- Paul was sent by the chief captain to Felix the governor.
- Felix allowed Paul some freedom in prison [Acts 24:23].
- Felix often talked with Paul for two years.
- Felix wanted a bribe from Paul.
- Felix did not accept Jesus Christ as His Lord during his chat with Paul.
- Felix was succeeded by another governor.

Exercise:
- Explain who a governor is to the child.
- Explain what a bribe is and why it is wrong to expect or give a bribe.
- Help the child to know that listening to God's words is not enough; we must believe and obey it.
- Help the child to realise the importance of accepting Jesus as Lord right now at the first opportunity and not later.
- Let the child know that he/she can be in a high post and still believe and serve Jesus.
- Let the child know that no position is permanent. Child should use his/her position the way that pleases God.
- Give the child the opportunity of accepting the Lord as his/her Saviour.

Parent/Teacher's additional note:

G is for Goliath, the giant killed by David, the little shepherd boy.

Read: 1 Samuel 17: 1-50

Points:
- Goliath was the leader of the Philistines who were fighting Israel.
- Goliath was a giant; he had six toes and six fingers on each hand/foot.
- Goliath had been a soldier since he was young.
- Goliath had big weapons and a man carrying his armour.
- Goliath insulted God Almighty.
- For many days Goliath was proud against God and his people.
- For many days Goliath frightened the Israelites on the battle field.
- David, the little shepherd boy was sent by his father to visit his brothers at war.
- David, the little shepherd boy had five stones and a sling.
- David, the little shepherd boy killed Goliath with one stone from the sling.

Exercise:
- Help the child to identify any fear he/she may have. To the child this is a Goliath.

- Help the child to realize that God hates a proud person.
- Explain to the child that every problem that looks like Goliath before the child can be destroyed.
- God is able to use even a small child to defeat Satan.
- Help the child to realize that at the mention of Jesus' Christ name and using the word of Satan will run away/flee.
- Explain to child that the Bible contains enough words to defeat any problem that the child has or may face in life.
- Explain to the child that in the name of Jesus Christ and the word of God, he/she can defeat every cause of fear.
- Help the child to learn one useful/applicable verse in the Bible.
- Pray with/for the child [Psalms 23:4, 46:1, 4:8, 9:10, 18:2, 34:4; Proverbs 18:10].
- Admonish child not to be a Goliath to others.

Note:

- *There is need to gain the child's trust before, during and after this session.*
- *Be sensitive and take any relevant action especially if the child's life or health is at risk e.g. school or neighbour's bullying, sexual or verbal assault in the home.*
- *Seek Godly and professional counselling if you do not know what to do or how to go about this.*

Parent/Teacher's additional note:

H is for the Hannah, the mother of Samuel.

Read: 1 Samuel 1: 1-28

Points:
- For many years after Hannah got married she couldn't have any child.
- Hannah was unhappy because she did not have a child.
- Another woman always laughed at and mocked her.
- Hannah still went to Shiloh, the house of God to worship.
- One day Hannah was alone in the temple and she cried to God in her heart.
- Hannah promised God that if He gave her a son, she would give him back to God.
- God heard Hannah and gave her many children, beginning with Samuel the Prophet of God.
- Hannah dedicated Samuel to God and sang a song of praise to God.

Exercise:

- Identify with child what or who makes him/her unhappy and give counsel.
- Pray with child believing God for a change for the better in the situation.

- Help the child to identify those things that can keep the child away from Church.
- Explain to the child that our problems should not keep us away from God's house or worship.
- Assure child that God will hear and answer him/her directly.
- Teach the child how to pray simple prayer appropriate for his/her age and encourage child to pray always especially in the time of trouble/problem.
- Encourage child to praise God by singing or telling others about God's love.
- Encourage child to keep any promises made to God or anyone else.
- Explain to child that God doesn't' like us mocking/bullying others who are less fortunate than them/ourselves.

Note:
- *There is need to gain the child's trust before, during and after this session.*
- *Parents/teachers please be sensitive to any indication of bullying at home, school or with neighbours and report/ deal with it appropriately.*

Parents/Teachers Manual

Parent/Teacher's additional note:

I is for is for Isaac, the son of Abraham.

Read: Genesis 18:1-15, 21: 1-8, 22:1-14.

Points:
- Isaac's parents were Abraham and Sarah.
- God promised to give Abraham and Sarah a son.
- For many years after they did not have a child of theirs.
- One day three strangers visited Abraham and Sarah.
- Abraham and Sarah fed these strangers who turned out to be angels.
- God reminded them of His promise of a son to them.
- A year later Sarah gave birth to a son and named him Isaac.
- Isaac was born when his parents were very old.
- Isaac's name means laughter.
- Isaac was a special child to his parents.
- Isaac often thought about God and spent time alone with God in the fields.
- Isaac married Rebecca.
- Isaac prayed that Rebecca would have a child.
- Isaac and Rebecca had a set of twins (Jacob and Esau).

Exercise:
- Let the child know that he/she is special to God and to the parents.

- Explain the child's name and help the child to learn how to correctly pronounce, spell and write his/her full name.
- Explain to child that God is always faithful no matter what.
- Let the child know that God always keeps His promise.
- Share with child any personal experience of God's faithfulness.
- The sun shines on the good and bad, the moon shines daily. Let the child know that so long as the sun and moon shine, child should be re-assured that God will remain faithful and keep His promises.
- Help the child to understand the importance of spending time alone with God anywhere and anytime for any request.
- Positively encourage the child to spend time talking to God.

Parent/Teacher's additional note:

J is for Jesus Christ, the only Son of God, our Saviour.

Read: John 3:16

Points:

- Jesus is the only Son of God.
- Jesus was conceived by the Holy Ghost, born of a virgin, lived and was crucified.
- He died and He rose on the 3rd day.
- Jesus gave His life on the cross so that (mention child's name) sins can be forgiven.
- Jesus leads (mention child's name) to the Father.
- Jesus lives in heaven now but the Holy Spirit lives in everyone who believe in Jesus Christ.
- Jesus will come back one day to take those who believe in Him to Heaven.
- All who believe in Jesus Christ as a Saviour are children of God.

Exercise:

- Help the child to understand the need for and, how to become born again or God's child.
- Say a simple sinner's prayer with the child e.g.

- Dear Lord Jesus, thank You for coming to this world. Thank You for loving *(mention child's name here)*. Thank You for dying for mention child's name). He/she loves You too Jesus. Jesus come and live in *(mention child's name)* heart from today. In Jesus Christ name we pray. Amen.
- Then re-assure child using his/her name that he/she is now a born again child of God.
- Encourage the child to share /tell his/her friends of this decision/ his/her new faith.
- Explain to the child for him/her to grow in the Lord, he/she will need to read the Bible and pray just as eating and drinking.

Parent/Teacher's additional note:

K is for King Asa, a king who loved God.

Read: 1 Kings 15:9–15.

Points:

- Asa was one of the Kings in Judah.
- Asa reigned for forty one years in Jerusalem.
- Asa did what was right in the sight of God.
- Asa followed in the good steps of his father David.
- Asa removed anything or anyone that did evil against God.
- Asa gave silver and gold for the work of God in the temple.
- Asa's heart was true to God all his life.

Exercise:
- Explain to the child God sees all he/she does.
- Explain to child that with Jesus' help child can live right before God.
- Identify with child any bad habit or thing that is against God.
- Explain why that habit is bad and wrong and against God.
- Encourage child to do away with anything that is evil or against God.
- Identify with child what gifts child can give or use for God's work.

- Encourage child to be truthful to God all through his/her life.
- Identify with child some good traits in you as the parent that the child can emulate.

Children learn best by parental example. How are you doing as a parent?

Parent/Teacher's additional note:

Parents/Teachers Manual

L is for Lydia, the seller of purple cloth.

Read: Acts 16:13-15

Points:

- Lydia was a trader (business woman).
- Lydia sold expensive clothes - purple clothes which are meant for royal people like kings, queens, princes and princesses.
- Lydia was a believer.
- Lydia found time whilst on business trip away from home to go to the fellowship that met by the river side.
- Lydia believed in Jesus Christ and was baptized.
- Lydia invited Paul to her home and always shared with people from her resources or from what she had.

Exercise:

- Discuss with child what he/she would like to become when he/she grows up.
- Help child to understand that whatever he/she grows up to become, he/she can still be a believer/ child of God, e.g. as a teacher, radiographer, nurse, accountant or doctor the child can pray for the sick.
- Remind child to remember to go to Church/Bible Club/

Sunday School when away from home e.g. on holidays to cousins/friends.
- Together with child discuss ways in which child *(mention child's name)* can share child's faith
- Identify with child what he/she can do to help others who are in need.
- Help the child to identify at least one person he/she will invite to the Sunday School or Bible club or Church.
- Identify with child what he/she can do to help his/her pastor/teacher e.g. pray or make them a card on their birthdays or always remember to say thank you to them.

Parents/Teachers Manual

Parent/Teacher's additional note:

M is for Moses, the most humble man on earth.

Read Exodus 2:1-2:15; 3:1-12

Points:

- The Israelites were slaves in Egypt.
- Moses was born when the king ordered all boys to be killed.
- Moses was very beautiful.
- Moses' life was spared by the Princess when she found him in a floating basket on the river.
- Moses was adopted and brought up as a Prince in Egypt.
- Moses had a speech problem – he stammered.
- Moses killed an Egyptian, then ran away to avoid death (being killed in return).
- God called Moses on Mount Horeb to return to Egypt and rescue His people.
- Moses was the most humble man that ever lived.
- Moses obeyed God and led the Israelites out of Egypt to the Promised Land of Canaan.

Exercise:

- Explain to the child what it means to be humble.
- Explain to the child - why it is nice to be humble.
- God is able to use child in spite of any weakness or sickness.

- Re-assure child that (mention child's name) is beautiful/handsome in your sight and that of God.
- Remind child using child's name that he/she has a purpose in God's plan for the world, in other words, he/she is useful/important to God and child's community.
- Find at least one beautiful/good thing about the child, mention it and commend it to the child.
- Let the child know that God is able use him/her in spite of any weakness.
- Play with the child a game that I call 'Where is God?'

Aim of the game is for child to know that:

- God is everywhere.
- God sees everyone, everywhere at the same time.
- No one can run away from God.

The Parent/ Teacher asks the child the question and the chid replies e.g.

PARENT : CHILD
Is GOD in the kitchen? Yes
Is GOD in the bedroom? Yes
Is GOD in our car? Yes
Is GOD in our Church? Yes etc.

The game can go on for as long as the child or parent want.

The game can be replayed with the parent answering the question now.

Parent/Teacher's additional note:

N is for Noah, the only righteous man on earth long time ago.

Read: Genesis 6:9-22.

Points:

- Noah was the only man that obeyed God in his time.
- The other people in the world at that time were wicked.
- God wasn't happy with the evil in the world.
- God decided to destroy the world.
- God spared Noah and his family.
- God told Noah to build the first big ship and zoo.
- The rains came and the whole world at that time was destroyed.
- Noah and his family were spared.

Exercise:

- Explain to the child what it means to be a righteous person.
- Help the child identify the animals and the birds that were in the ark and relate it to child's visit to the zoo.
- Help the child to know that God cares for our planet and the animals too.

- Help the child to identify how he/she can hear God. E.g. audibly, in their dreams, through the Word, as he/she reads the Bible etc.
- Explain to the child why he/she should obey God.
- Explain to the child that God sees and knows every good or bad person on earth at any time.
- God rewards righteousness.
- God protects the righteous people.

Parents/Teachers Manual

Parent/Teacher's additional note:

O is for Onesimus, the profitable runaway slave.

Read: Philemon 10 -21.

Points:

- Onesimus was a slave of Philemon.
- Onesimus ran away from Philemon his master.
- Onesimus met Paul whilst on the run.
- Onesimus gave his life to Jesus Christ.
- Onesimus became useful to Paul and Philemon his master.

Exercise:

Explain to the child :
- Who a slave is.
- That a slave is always ruled by his master or what it means to be a slave.
- A slave is not free except the master sets him/her free.
- Which things/objects/habits that can enslave him/her.
- How to avoid becoming a slave to Satan or the wrong people e.g. Keeping and being a good friend always, avoiding people who want him/her to do wrong things, avoiding being in bad and wrong places, telling the truth always etc.

- Help the child to know that there is freedom in Jesus Christ only.
- God will help any believer (child of God) *(mention child's name)* to be useful to Him and His people.
- Find out who child's hero is and why.

Parent/Teacher's additional note:

P is for Peter, the leader of the disciples.

Read: Matthew 4:18-22; Acts 2:1-42.

Points:

- Jesus chose 12 men to be his disciples (be with him).
- Peter was one of them.
- Peter was a fisherman when he met Jesus.
- Peter was always with Jesus.
- Peter walked once on the sea towards Jesus.
- Peter once caught a fish with money in the fish's mouth.
- Peter became the leader of the disciples after Jesus went to heaven.

Exercise:

- Remind child using child's name that God is able to use him/her in whatever job he/she does.
- Together with child, identify ways of being with Jesus today e.g. reading the Bible, going to Bible clubs/Church, singing to God, telling our friends about Jesus and praying.
- Explain to the child that God is still providing for His own today.

- Together with child, identify qualities of a good leader and the ones the child is already demonstrating and commend him/her for it.
- Find out from child what he/she wants to do when he/she grows up and why.
- Pray with child on the identified skills/talents.

Parent/Teacher's additional note:

Q is for Queen of Sheba, King Solomon's guest

Read: I Kings 10:1- 13

Points:

- Queen Sheba was the Queen of Sheba.
- Queen Sheba heard about King Solomon's wisdom.
- Queen Sheba was willing to learn from another King.
- Queen Sheba visited King Solomon to learn about his Godly wisdom.
- Queen Sheba gave King Solomon many gifts.
- Queen Sheba returned to her country after this visit.

Exercise:

- Encourage the child to be humble before God and man.
- Child should be willing to positively learn from others if and when need be.
- Child should be encouraged to help others in need.
- The Holy Spirit lives in the heart of those who have accepted Jesus Christ as their Lord.
- The Holy Spirit in the believer gives us Godly wisdom as we yield to Him.
- It is nice to give good gifts especially to those we learn from e.g. a handmade card for his/her teacher at school /Sunday school.

Parent/Teacher's additional note:

R is for Rebecca, the mother of twins.

Read: Genesis 25:19 - 27

Points:

- Isaac prayed to God for children.
- Rebecca was the wife of Isaac, Abraham's son.
- God allowed Rebecca to become pregnant.
- Rebecca prayed to God whilst she was pregnant.
- God spoke to Rebecca about her forthcoming children.
- God gave Isaac and Rebecca twins.
- Though born by the same parents and on the same day, Esau was different from Jacob.
- Esau was hairy, had red colour skin and was a hunter.
- Jacob had a smooth skin and was a home lover/maker.

Exercise:

- Remind child that no two people can be exactly the same.
- God has a plan for each one, even twins.
- Help the child to understand ways in which twins may or may not look alike e.g.
- Each person has a kitchen (placenta) whilst growing inside their mother's womb.

Parents/Teachers Manual

- Twins that share the same kitchen inside their mother's womb tend to look alike (identical twins) and are of same sex.
- Twins that have different kitchen inside their mother's womb don't look alike (non identical twins), they may be the same sex like Esau and Jacob and at other times be different sex e.g. a boy and a girl.
- Ask if child knows any twins and pray for child and the twins.

Parent/Teacher's additional note:

Parents/Teachers Manual

S is for the Shepherds, who watched their flocks by night.

Read: Luke 2:8–19

Points:

- Some shepherds were watching their flock by night outside Bethlehem.
- Suddenly there was a bright light around them and the shepherds were afraid.
- An angel of the Lord appeared to them and calmed their fears.
- The angel told them the 'good news' of Jesus' birth which was that Jesus the Saviour and greatest shepherd of mankind had been born in Bethlehem.
- Other heavenly hosts appeared singing songs of praise to the Lord.
- The shepherds immediately left their flock after the angel left to find and worship Jesus the king.

Exercise:

- Identify with child a good news that child has ever had e.g. a new toy, a new baby in the family, a new family house or car etc. Ask the child how it made the child to feel.
- Jesus Christ is the good and best news to mankind.

- Using John 3:16 and Revelation 3:20, in an uncomplicated way, briefly explain salvation and give the child the opportunity to be saved.
- Encourage child to worship God always by praying, singing, reading the Bible and fellowshipping with other believers (Hebrews 10:25).
- Encourage the child to share this 'good news' with friends, family and neighbours.

Parent/Teacher's additional note:

T is for Timothy, Paul's son in the Lord.

Read: 2 Timothy 1:3-7

Points:

- Timothy's mother was Eunice.
- Timothy's grandmother was Lois.
- Timothy was taught by his mother and grandmother.
- They taught Timothy to believe in God.
- Timothy loved God.
- Young Timothy's mentor (role model) was Paul.
- Timothy became a Pastor/leader as a young man.

Exercise:

- Tell the child about his/her or any grandmother using any pictures if available.
- Together with the child draw or make a family tree explaining to child who a great grandmother is.
- Together with child and using Granny's picture (if available), talk about the good deeds of child's grandparents especially the grandmother.
- Identify ways to bless grannies, e.g. pray for them, thank them, obey them and remember their birthdays.
- Explain to the child who a pastor or leader is.

- Ask child if he/she loves God and identify together, ways of showing his/her love to God e.g. by obeying Him etc.
- Identify with child his/her role model and why child has chosen that mentor.

Parent/Teacher's additional note:

U is for Uriah the Hittite, one of the mighty men in King David's army.

Read: 2 Samuel 11:6- 21, 23:39

Points:

- Uriah was a strong man.
- Uriah was a soldier in King David's army.
- Uriah was one of the top 30 soldiers in King David's army.
- Uriah was an upright, honest and disciplined man.
- Uriah fought in many battles.
- Uriah respected the Ark of Covenant more than his comfort.
- Uriah obeyed his commander.
- Uriah got killed whilst at war.

Exercise:

- Together with child identify the uniform of soldiers and relate each to the weapons of our warfare *[Ephesians 6:10 – 17]*.
- Encourage the child not to be afraid of soldiers who are normally meant to maintain peace in a country and fight the enemies of their country.
- Everyone including child who has given his/her life to Jesus

is in God's army and in God can be mighty as Uriah.
- Let the child know that sometimes in the battle some brave soldiers still die.
- Let the child know that soldiers are always required to obey their commanders so we must also obey God.
- Together with child pray for the safety of the soldiers and their families.
- Pray for children whose parents have died in a battle.

Note:
Should this lesson be taught to any child with a military background, sensitivity to the heart cries of the child must be identified and dealt with.

Parents/Teachers Manual

Parent/Teacher's additional note:

V is for Virgin Mary, the mother of Jesus Christ.

Read: Matthew 1:18 -27

Points:

- Angel Gabriel appeared to Mary whilst she was alone.
- Angel Gabriel told Mary she will soon become pregnant.
- Angel Gabriel told Mary that she will have a baby boy.
- Mary was to call him Jesus meaning Saviour.
- Mary believed the words of God.
- Soon after that, Mary noticed she was pregnant.
- Mary had her baby in a manger in Bethlehem.

Exercise:

Explain to child that:

- Angels are messengers of God.
- Angels can appear in any form – e.g. as another unknown person talking to us or giving us God's words or instructions.
- Every child who has given his/her life to Jesus has a guarding angel *[Matthew 18:10]*.
- God sends His angels to guard us, protect us and deliver us in times of trouble as well as bring us good news from God.

- We are not to worship angels.
- Angels return to God once they complete thier mission.
- God still uses His angels today.

Parent/Teacher's additional note:

Parents/Teachers Manual

W is for the Wise Men, who came to visit baby Jesus in the manger.

Read: Matthew 2:1-12

Points:

- Wise men from the East noticed a bright star in the sky.
- They recognized from the bright star that a king had been born.
- They followed the star from the East to Israel.
- They asked King Herod if he knew about the new-born king and where to find him.
- They traced the star to a manger in Bethlehem where Jesus was born.
- They gave Jesus presents.
- They worshipped Jesus and after that they returned home.

Exercise:

Explain to the child that the wise person is one who:

- Has asked Jesus into his/her life.
- Tell others about Jesus [Proverbs 11:30]
- Seeks Jesus and obeys Jesus.

Using John 3:16 and Revelation 3:20, in an uncomplicated way, briefly explain salvation and give the child the opportunity to be saved.
- Pray together with child and ask God to grant special wisdom to child [James 1:5-6]
- Together with child thank God for this wisdom in advance.
- Together with child, identify what we can give to Jesus after giving Him our life e.g. our time in prayers, singing, using our gifts and talents for God and for other people.

Parents/Teachers Manual

Parent/Teacher's additional note:

X is for X-Ray, God can see inside of my heart.

Read: Jeremiah 17:9 -10.

Points:

- X-Ray can see the bones and the inside of people but only God can see what is inside the heart of everyone including child's name.
- God can see what (mention child's name) is thinking.
- God can see if (mention child's name) believes God.
- God can see if (mention child's name) obeys God.
- God can see if (mention child's name) walk with God.
- The heart is the engine that works the body.

Exercise:

- Help child to identify ways of having and keeping good thoughts e.g. being careful with what child sees, watches what he/she reads and think about, having and being a good friend, being careful about where the child goes and what he/she does etc..
- Explain to the child that God can see everything inside the child's mind, thoughts and actions.

- God can see inside the child's body and God can heal the child from any sickness or disease.
- Help the child to learn at least one memory verse from the Bible.
- Let the child know that we need to have a good heart because our thoughts and actions come from it.
- Pray with the child for healing of anyone you know needs healing.

Parent/Teacher's additional note:

Y is for YAWEH, another name for/of GOD.

Read: Exodus 3:13- 15

Points:

- God has many names.
- One of them is YAHWEH meaning 'I am that I am'.
- We need to respect God's name.
- We need to be careful how, where and when we use God's name.
- God answers when we call on His name anytime, anywhere and for anything.

Exercise:

- Help the child to list the other names of God.
- Help the child to understand the importance of each of God's names mentioned.
- Help child to list the attributes of God relevant to his/her age.
- Together with child identify what times child can call on God – anytime, anywhere – and, for what - anything.
- Together with child praise God using God's name listed above.

- Identify any praise or prayer point in the life / family and pray over it.
- Teach and help the child to thank God in advance for answered prayers.

Parent/Teacher's additional note:

Z is for Zacchaeus, the short man and tax collector who lived in Jericho.

Read: Luke 19:1-10

Points:

- Zacchaeus lived in Jericho.
- Zacchaeus was a tax collector.
- Zacchaeus was a rich man but Zacchaeus was a bad man who took too much money from the people as tax.
- Zacchaeus was a very short man.
- Zacchaeus wanted to see Jesus.
- Zacchaeus climbed the tree in order to see Jesus as He passed by.
- Jesus called Zacchaeus to come down from the tree he was on.
- Jesus visited Zacchaeus in his home.
- Zacchaeus confessed his sins to Jesus and Jesus forgave him.
- Jesus will forgive us of the bad things we do if we ask Him.

Exercise:

- Explain to the child what tax is and who a tax collector is.
- Identify with child the good causes for which the tax paid is used for e.g. running schools, hospitals for the sick, pay

- the police that ensures our safety, fire fighters who put away fires, build roads and other communal social services.
- Help the child to understand how to say sorry to God and people when he/she is in the wrong.
- Re-assure child that God through Jesus will forgive us of all the bad things we do if we sincerely tell Him we are sorry.
- Encourage child to forgive himself/herself after he/she has asked God for forgiveness.
- Let the child know that seeing Jesus or believing in Jesus no longer depends on anyone's height or size.
- Let the child know that Jesus loves us in spite of our sins.
- Give room for the child to say sorry to God and people whom he/she might have wronged.
- Give the child the opportunity to accept Jesus Christ in his/her life.

Well done parent/teacher. Good job!

May the promise of God in Proverbs 22:6 be ours in Jesus' name. Amen!

Parent/Teacher's additional note:

Parents/Teachers Manual

OPPORTUNITY TO BECOME A CHRISTIAN

Dear Father in heaven,

Thank you for the privilege of reading this book. Indeed I have sinned and come short of Your glory. I am grateful to You for sending Jesus Christ into this world to come to die on the cross of Calvary for me. I believe in my heart that Jesus Christ paid for my sins, past, present and future. I believe Jesus Christ was buried and on the third day He rose from the dead. I believe that Jesus Christ will come back again. I confess with my mouth and I accept Him now to be my Lord.

Master, Saviour, Brother, and Friend, I ask in Your mercy for the infilling of the Holy Spirit so that with His help, I can live a victorious life becoming all that You have ordained me to be in Jesus' name. I pray with thanksgiving. Amen.

If after reading this book you said the above prayer and became born-again, Congratulations! You are Born Again is a booklet for those who have done so through reading this book. It is a free booklet that we would like you to have. In it, the frequently asked questions are answered and this will get you on the way to growing in your newfound faith in God. You can download this free booklet from our website: www.protokospublishers.com

You may also contact any of the organisations listed at the end of the book.

I look forward to hearing from you soon.
O. Ola – Ojo (2011)

Parents/Teachers Manual

Other Books By The Author:

Provocation, Prayer and Praise
(December 2004 & 2009)

Complimentary to The Christian and Infertility this book focuses on the story of an infertile woman in the Bible, her provocations, prayer and praise. Whatever makes you incomplete, unfulfilled, less than whom God made you to be, whatever issue of life that the enemy uses to provoke you calls for prayer.

Key features include:
- Some known medical reasons for infertility in the women.
- Why Hannah went to the house of God in spite of her barrenness.
- Is it true that the husband is much more than 10 sons to the infertile woman?
- When, where and how to address the source/cause of your provocation.
- God's part and your part in that promise.
- God is able to met that humanly impossible need of yours.
- A time to celebrate and praise God.
-

Book Details:
Paperback: 128 pages
Language English
ISBN-13: 978-0-9557898-3-0

Review:
A Reader from London, 7 Jan 2006 on Amazon.co.uk
An excellent easy to read and understand book. The principles shared in this book though primarily are for those trying for a baby could as well be applied to any area of hurt and un-fulfilment.

 :www.protokospublishers.com

ABC of People and Things in the Bible

The Christian and Infertility
(December 2004 & 2009)

The Christian and Infertility addresses one of the often neglected needs of Christian couples. It gives an insight into infertility from the biblical and medical perspectives. It is written not only for potential fruitful couples but for pastors, family and friends of these couples. It is written that the Body of Christ might be fully equipped to know and support couples who are facing the challenge of infertility at present.

Key features include:
- Childleness in the Bible and lessons to learn;
- Some possible physical, medical and environmental causes of infertility;
- Some known spiritual causes of infertility;
- The man and low sperm count;
- Some of the available treatment optons in the UK;
- Choice of fertility treatment;
- Should a christian professional be involved in fertility treatment?

Book Details:
Paperback: 146 pages
Language English
ISBN-13: 978-0-9557898-2-3

Review:
A reviewer from Glen Burnie, USA, 29 Oct 2007 on Amazon.co.uk'
The book is a great eye-opener for all. It sheds light on infertility from the medical and spiritual angle. This gives the reader a balance because i believe every human being is made up of both physical and spiritual part. To get a balance in life, the two parts must be well fed. One must not concentrate on the spiritual and neglect the physical part. The book also reminds us that God has a way of sorting us out.... The book is quite inspiring. I will recommend this book to everybody trusting God for any form of blessing from God to go get one and apply it to his or her situation. It will definitely bless you and yours'.

 :www.protokospublishers.com

Parents/Teachers Manual

Obstetrics and Gynaecology Ultrasound -
A Self-Assessment Guide
June 2005 Churchill Elsevier Publishers, UK.

This self-assessment guide is a structured questions and answer book that develops the reader's understanding capability using a simple method in treating related topics. Clinical indications are presented with their corresponding ultrasound findings using appropriate illustrations. A case study approach is followed; presenting the clinical and ethical dilemmas that might arise whilst encouraging students to think. The aim is to reinforce theoretical knowledge within a clinical environment.

Book details:
- Over 600 high-resolution ultrasound images
- Cover a wide spectrum of ultrasound curriculum.
- Includes a detailed study of fertility.
- Aids quick understanding of subject matter.
- 468 pages.

ISBN-10: 0443064628
ISBN-13: 978-0443064623

Review:
"...This excellent new book is a study guide… This is an attractive paperback that should be essential reading for trainee obstetric and gynaecological sonographers, whether they are radiographers or radiology or obstetric trainees. It will be of particular value to those preparing for the RCOG/RCR Diploma in Advanced Obstetric Ultrasound and to specialist registrars in obstetrics and gynaecology undertaking special skills modules in fetal medicine, gynaecological ultrasound and infertility..."

The Obstetrician & Gynaecologist, www.rcog.org.uk/togonline
Book reviews 2006

Reviewer **Ann Harper MD FRCPI FRCOG.**
Consultant Obstetrician and Gynaecologist
Royal Jubilee Maternity Service, Belfast., UK

 :www.protokospublishers.com

GOOD MUMS, BAD MUMS
(June 2005 & 2009)

This is in two parts, the main chapter that can be used for personal or group study, and an accompanying exercise section. The privileged position of a mother is in her being a co-creator with God and bringing forth life (lives). This book compliments one of God's previous revelations to me as contained in the book titled Good Dads, Bad Dads'. While the father could be likened to the pilot of the family plane, the mother can be likened to the force behind the plane – positive or negative. Good mothers are not only co-creators with God, they also do nurture as well as nourish their children physically, emotionally and spiritually.

Keys Features:
- Were all the mothers in the Bible god mothers?
- Lessons from the strengths and weakness of seven mothers.
- Be encouraged - you are not alone in the assignment of motherhood.
- Be motivated in the areas of your strengths.
- Learn ways of supporting your husband and children.

Book Details:
Paperback: 162 pages
Language English
ISBN-13: 978-0-9557898-1-6

Review:
I appreciate the author's method of writing. It is always exciting holding her book to read. Personally, 'Good Mums, Bad Mums' has been a blessing to me in no small measure. The book is rich, it is loaded with physical and spiritual uplifting subjects. To all existing and potential mothers, this book is a MUST read. At the end of every chapter there is an exercise to do that will help in re-examining your life spiritually and in other ways. I encourage all women to get and use this book as a guide in raising their children. You will be glad you did.

Pastor Mrs T Adegoke
Freedom Arena
London, UK

 :www.protokospublishers.com

Parents/Teachers Manual

To the Bride with Love
(2007 & 2009)

Every wise woman preparing to get married knows she will need sound advice, practical tips and solid, heartfelt prayers, of those who have travelled on the road she is about to journey on. In this book, 10 women of different age groups, from different backgrounds and cultures who wedded under various circumstances, individually share their experience with the bride in an intimate, very candid and unforgettable way.

Book details:
Paperback: 108 pages
Language English
ISBN-13: 978-0-9557898-4-7

To the Bride with Love is the perfect bride's evergreen companion. The content is suitable, relevant and applicable even decades after the wedding day.

To the Bride with Love is an ideal wedding gift on its own. It can also accompany any other gift (big or small) that you have for the bride but take this hint... the bride will keep thanking you for the book years and years after.

Reviews:
'One of the best', 19 Jul 2008 on Amazon.com
Sade Olaoye "clare4good" (United Kingdom)
This book has really helped my marriage from the onset as I got it as a wedding gift, God bless the giver. It's a must read for relationship improvement and God's guidance. I recommend it for people to get it for themselves, moreover as a great blessing for someone else in love. "To the Bride with Love"

Review by **Oyinlola Odunlami** CEO.
Shallom Bookshop, London UK
The writing style of Oluwakemi is unique, peculiar and distinct to herself. I recommend To the Bride with Love to wives, wives to be, mothers, mentors, youth leaders and workers. Why? The clarity, the focus and the intent of this book is so empowering, encouraging and enlightening that it will definitely mould or re mould a life to achieve its purpose. The truth is, there are very few

books that have depth as well as help you to achieve your goals and arrive at your destination. Many books tend to excite you but have no depth; you read and you forget; they do not really change you but this book, To the Bride with Love will definitely leave a word in your spirit and move you to your next level!

I believe that this is also a book that pastors will find useful as a manual for marriage counselling, because many books on marriage focus mostly on what you as an individual can gain, your own personal satisfaction while little is said about the sacrifices involved and their importance. As my pastor usually says, it is important to learn from those who have gone ahead, understand why some were successful and others weren't, so that we won't fall where they fell, rather, we would gain more speed, achieve our goals and thereby glorify Christ.

So, I invite you not only to get a copy of this life-changing manual for yourself, but also to put it into as many hands as you can afford to, for then the world will definitely benefit and your life will be a blessing to many.

 :www.protokospublishers.com

Parents/Teachers Manual

Refuge Under His Wings

"an exhaustive analysis of the Book of Ruth in the Bible. The author combines her deep Christian conviction and excellent knowledge of the Holy Scriptures to produce a must read for every Christian, married or single. The book is interspaced with beautifully written prayers, which enables the reader to pause, pray and meditate on the revelations received... The book is also loaded with poetry like 'Thy will be done oh Lord' for those who may be facing an uncertain future or on a cross road of decisions."

Dr E B Ekpo MD, FRCP
Queen Elizabeth Hospital, Christian Fellowship,
Woolwich, London. UK

"...[a] ...spiritually sound book... a fine work of thoughtful reading and study... I therefore recommend it to every Christian, married or single....
Pat Roach Senior Pastor
New Covenant Church.
Wandsworth Branch, London. UK.

Book details:
Paperback: 100 pages
Language English
ISBN-10: 095578980X
ISBN-13: 978-0955789809

Review:
This book feeds the soul. Most of all I loved the poetry. It gives you time to savour the thoughts as a reader. There is a good mix of poetry and prose. To look at the story of Ruth in depth gave good spiritual food. You can pause and take it in at your own pace. The meditation on Psalm 121 was good also. There's nothing like reading a Psalm slowly and meditating on its contents. The author's own reflections allow you to see the book through someone else's eyes. A good read.

Gaby Richards, London, UK.

 :www.protokospublishers.com

GRACE OR WORKS

This book makes you examine a lot of issues in your life, family relationships in particular, that you may have taken for granted or totally ignored. As conveyed right from the rhetorical question posed in the title, Grace or Works, the author stirs you towards asking yourself pertinent questions, thinking through for answers and even getting solutions for unresolved problems.

Have you heard of prodigal wives, husbands, mothers or prodigal fathers? This book identifies and defines them clearly. For anyone experiencing a crises in their relationship with such prodigal family members, this book, which is based on the parable of the "Prodigal son" in Luke 15:11-32 is a one-stop resource material to meet your counselling needs. And just in case you happen to be the prodigal who has caused your relatives much sorrow, there is hope for you in this book.

Interspersed with prayers for you by the author and specific prayers that you can say for yourself, as well as poems to comfort and inspire you, Grace or Works not only asks you questions, it helps you make and maintain the right choices.

Book details:
Paperback: 122 pages
Language English
ISBN-13: 978-0-9557898-5-4

:www.protokospublishers.com

Parents/Teachers Manual

THERE IS A REWARD FOR PARENTING

Man may claim that the conception of a particular child was accidental, but in God's eyes every child is in His plan and has a purpose and mission to fulfil here on earth. As a parent, teacher, church or community leader, how are you treating the children in your care?

God does not sleep nor slumber; are you sure you are doing what He expects of you as a parent or children's Sunday school teacher? What kind of reward do you expect from Him?

There is a Reward for Parenting provides a lot of answers and food for thought, using scriptural principles to show you how to ensure a good reward from God in the unique assignment of parenting and child care.

As characteristic of Oluwakemi Ola-Ojo's previous books, there is a free gift of her poems at the end of this book also, to add value to the content of the main text – making it two books for the price of one!

Book details:
Paperback: 88 pages
Language English
ISBN 978-0-9557898-6-1

Review:
The book is lovely, inspiring, very educative both spiritually and secularly.

M.F.Owoeye
Lagos- Nigeria

:www.protokospublishers.com

Let's Reason Together ...Youths' A-Z (Book 1)

According to the United Nations demographic statistics, the global youth population, ranging in age from 15 to 24 years, today stands at more than 1.5 billion, representing about 22 percent or a fifth of the world's 6.8 billion people inhabiting the earth. In developing nations where a greater number of this group resides, the youth population sometimes gets as high as 60% or more of the total population of such nations!

Since it is also globally accepted that the youth of any nation forms the strength of that nation, economically, militarily and/or otherwise, it is imperative that this group of people cannot be overlooked.

It is against this backdrop that the book, **LET'S REASON TOGETHER – YOUTH'S A-Z** is a timely one that is set to address the various issues that affect young people as well as their vision and aspirations. Since the primary goal of young people is to live full lives in their societies, this book examines specific elements that would help them in this process. It covers a wide range of issues from the sublime such as attitude, choices, education, health and xenophobia to the seemingly mundane such as dreams, integrity and vacation etc.

Oluwakemi Ola-Ojo has written from her wealth of experience both in the medical field as well as from a spiritual point of view and it is evident that a lot of research work was put into writing this book. Irrespective of your age and/or religious persuasion, this book will inform and guide you.

Book details:
Paperback: 316 pages
Language English
ISBN 978-0-9557898-7-8

Reviews:
This is the most wonderful piece of youth work I have ever seen, capturing diverse situations and circumstances peculiar to youths. The work is thorough, educative and spiritually exhilarating. It is a must have for every youth worker to use, either in group discussions, seminars or straightforward teaching. This piece of work will yet raise the gospel abroad.
Dr M Akindele, Consultant Paediatrician, London, UK

This is a must read for the youths and anyone that deals with teenagers. All Sunday school staff will benefit from this book.
Deaconess B. Josiah. London, UK

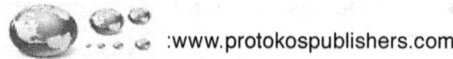 :www.protokospublishers.com

Let's Reason Together ...Youths' A-Z (Book 2)

According to the United Nations demographic statistics, the global youth population, ranging in age from 15 to 24 years, today stands at more than 1.5 billion, representing about 22 percent or a fifth of the world's 6.8 billion people inhabiting the earth. In developing nations where a greater number of this group resides, the youth population sometimes gets as high as 60% or more of the total population of such nations!

Since it is also globally accepted that the youth of any nation forms the strength of that nation, economically, militarily and/or otherwise, it is imperative that this group of people cannot be overlooked.

It is against this backdrop that the book, LET'S REASON TOGETHER – YOUTH'S A-Z is a timely one that is set to address the various issues that affect young people as well as their vision and aspirations. Since the primary goal of young people is to live full lives in their societies, this book examines specific elements that would help them in this process. It covers a wide range of issues from the sublime such as anger, drugs, examination, homosexuality, jealousy and rejection to the seemingly mundane such as growth, ignorance and youth etc.

Oluwakemi Ola-Ojo has written from her wealth of experience both in the medical field as well as from a spiritual point of view and it is evident that a lot of research work was put into writing this book.

Irrespective of your age and/or religious persuasion, this book will inform and guide you. I recommend it to youths as well as parents and every person working with young people i.e. Sunday school teachers, youth leaders and pastors and social workers.

Book details:
Paperback: 322 pages
Language English
ISBN 978-0-9557898-9-2

 :www.protokospublishers.com

Parents/Teachers Manual

ABC of PEOPLE and THINGS in the BIBLE

This Workbook 'ABC of People and Things in the Bible' is specifically written for the 6-8 year old as a corresponding tool to help the child learn and practice the lessons taught from the book, My ABC of People and Things in the Bible. It provides a series of basic do-it-yourself activities such as reading, writing and drawing.

The workbook is a perfect teaching aid that enables the child to express him/herself and helps the parent/teacher to identify the depth of the child's understanding or otherwise of the lessons taught.

Book details:
Paperback: 64 pages
Language English
ISBN 978-1-908015-05-1

:www.protokospublishers.com

GOOD DADS, BAD DADS

This is a timeless book for men of all generations. It is very pragmatic, informative and honest in its outlook and aims to be some resource of great support and guidance to fathers specifically and men in general.

It tackles such issues as showing favouritism, unconditional love, keeping pledges, providing for the family, building an altar of worship, obedience to God's voice and the importance of leadership in the home among others.

It is a very good indicator for men who want to ensure that peace, love and orderliness reign supreme in their homes and all other endeavours of life they are involved in. It is by no means exhaustive in its nature but acts as a pointer to the ageless truths found in the Bible. It challenges men to be all that they can be for the good of the society they live in and most of all the best fathers any children may ever desire to have. It is based on some Biblical characters, all of whom are very different one from the other with their flaws and areas of excellence in order that the good father today might eschew their short-comings and pursue those aspects of these biblical characters that are worthy.

To ensure that fathers continually transform their lives, there is an accompanying workbook to stimulate them and to keep the nuggets found in this book close to their hearts which in turn reflects in the way they live their lives.

Book details:
Paperback: 230 pages
Language English
ISBN 978-1-908015-00-6

"Just a note to say that the book 'Good Dads Bad Dads' is a powerful and thought-provoking book".

Prof A. I. Sodeye - United Kingdom

"To start with, I find the book pleasurable to read and understand. In my opinion the book is prophetic in that for individuals who are spiritually inclined, there is a conviction in a way that as you read along you tend to feel that this is not just a book discussing a topic.

The book is very engaging. It provides avenue for readers to reflect and take stock as they read along. Not only that, as a pastor I realise that most of the fatherly problems were highlighted maturedly though factually. The author provides us the opportunity to receive fresh insights from what is practicable and on-going in human affairs - duties and responsibilities of fathers. Additionally the book is timely in that we have many absent-fathers presently, which if they were opportuned to read or hear from someone who had read the book, at least the number of the run-away fathers, or absentees could have reduced.

The book is filled with wisdom and encouragement for anyone doing well as a father, simultaneously for those who are not really there yet, hope, contact details and prayers of repentance are offered.

I salute the author for being able to communicate effectively on a sensitive topic such as this one. The book, Good dads, Bad dads is not judgemental or sentimental, but is one of the books which is culturally relevant and once read, you will like to read it again."

Pastor Isaac Ajibolorunrin,
Christ The Lord Tabernacle, UK

 :www.protokospublishers.com

GOOD DADS, BAD DADS (Work Book)

This is a timeless book for men of all generations. It is very pragmatic, informative and honest in its outlook and aims to be some resource of great support and guidance to fathers specifically and men in general.

It tackles such issues as showing favouritism, unconditional love, keeping pledges, providing for the family, building an altar of worship, obedience to God's voice and the importance of leadership in the home among others.

It is a very good indication for men who want to ensure that peace, love and orderliness reign supreme in their homes and all other endeavours of life they are involved in. It is not at all exhaustive in its nature but acts as a pointer to the ageless truths found in the Bible. It challenges men to be all that they can be for the good of the society they live in and most of all the best fathers any children may ever desire to have.

To ensure that fathers continually transform lives, this is the accompanying workbook to stimulate them and to keep the nuggets found close to their hearts which in turn reflects in the way they live their lives.

Book details:
Paperback: 152 pages
Language English
ISBN 978-1-908015-01-3

COMING OUT SOON

- **A.B.C. OF PEOPLE AND THINGS IN THE BIBLE BOOK 2**
- **A.B.C. OF PLACES IN THE BIBLE BOOKS 1 & 2**

USEFUL ADDRESSES & WEBSITES

Care for the Family
PO Box 488
Cardiff
CF15 7YY
Tel: (029) 2081 0800
Fax: (029) 2081 4089
Email: mail@cff.org.uk
Website: www.care-for-the-family.org.uk OR www.cff.org.uk
Care for the Family aims to promote strong family life and to help those hurting because of family breakdown. Their heart is to come alongside people in the good times and in the tough times – bringing hope, compassion and some practical, down-to-earth help and encouragement.

Children Evangelism Ministry Inc
P.O. Box 4480
Ilorin, Kwara State,
Nigeria.
Tel: +234 31 222199
E-mail: cem@ilorin.skannet.com OR cem562000@yahoo.com
Children Evangelism Ministry Inc is a ministry that reaches out with the Gospel to children before and after birth. The ministry teaches and equips parents, teachers and coordinators of Sunday Schools and Children's Clubs. They also have and hold Children's Clubs, conferences and training seminars.

Focus on the Family
Tel: 1-800 - 232 6459
Website: www.family.org
Focus on the Family cooperates with the Holy Spirit in disseminating the Gospel of Jesus Christ to as many people as possible, and, specifically, to accomplish that objective by helping to preserve traditional values and the institution of the family.

Open Gate
2 Union Road
Croydon
CR0 2XU.
Tel: 0208 665 5533
Fax: 0208 684 7233
e-mail: opengate@yahoo.co.uk
         alteschool@yahoo.co.uk
Open Gate Provides a preventative and supplementary educational facility for youths at risk of permanent exclusion. We aim at empowering and connecting the youths for the future. We provide support for the family and the community.

Protokos Publishers
P.O. Box 48424
London
SE15 2YL
www.protokospublishers.com
Protokos Publishers provides various resources for the family. We publish many life's enlightening, informative and motivational must read books. With each of our books, you are guaranteed a 24/7 counsellor by your side on the subject.

The Shepherd's Ministries
5 Brookehowse Road
Bellingham
London SE6 3TJ, UK
Tel/Fax: +44 208 698 7222
Email: info@theshepherdsministries.org
Website: www.theshepherdsministries.org
The Shepherd's Ministries helps to bring children into an experience of worshipping God in truth and in spirit; give children a world-view based on God's word and mission and helps children to exercise their gifts in local and global missions.

Teenagers' Outreach Ministries (TOM) Inc.
Plot 85
Ladi Kwali Ext. Layout,
P.O.Box 16
Kwali, Abuja.
Nigeria.
Tel- 02082933730
Fax-02082933731
Nigeria - 08037044195, 07081860407
Email- tominthq@yahoo.co.uk
Website -www.tominternational.org
The Teenagers' Outreach Ministries (TOM) Inc. has a vision of leading today's teenager to Christ. This forms the foundation on which we mould their character in line with the word of God, thereby equipping them to fulfil their God ordained roles in life.

Total Woman Ministries
The Total Woman Ministries,
3 Herringham Road
Thames Wharf Barrier,
Charlton,
London
SE7 8NJ.
Tel: 020 8293 3730
Fax: 020 8293 3731
Email: admin@totalwomanministries.org
Website:www.totalwomanministries.org
Total Woman Ministries by God's grace has the sole vision of reaching out to women of all categories *(married, single, separated, divorced, young, middle-aged or elderly)*.

United Christian Broadcasting UCB
P.O. Box 255, Stoke on Trent,
ST4 8YY, England
Among other forms of spreading the Gospel, UCB prints The Word For Today – a free daily devotional reading available for residents in the UK and Republic of Ireland

IN USA:
www.eCounseling.com
Tel Number: 1-866-268-6735

Dear Reader,

Thank you for your time and resources committed to supporting this writing ministry. Please help to tell others about how much the Lord has blessed you reading this book.

You will certainly be blessed by the other books written by Oluwakemi, so why not visit www.protokospublishers.com and place an order today.

It will equally be appreciated if you can help to write a few sentences review of the book on www.amazon.com and / or on www.protokospublishers.com.

Please note that all our books are easily available on our website and other good bookshops.

God bless you as you do.
Management
Protokos Publishers.

www.ingramcontent.com/pod-product-compliance
Lightning Source LLC
Chambersburg PA
CBHW071006080526
44587CB00015B/2365